I Wonder Why

The Telephone Rings

and Other Questions About Communication

Richard Mead

Kingfisher

NEW YORK

KINGFISHER
Larousse Kingfisher Chambers Inc.
95 Madison Avenue
New York, New York 10016

First edition 1996
10 9 8 7 6 5 4 3 2 1
Copyright © Larousse plc 1996

LIBRARY OF CONGRESS CATALOGING-IN-PUBLICATION DATA
Mead, Richard
I wonder why the telephone rings and other questions
about communication / Richard Mead.—1st American ed.
    p.   cm.—(I wonder why)
    Includes Index.
Summary: Questions and answers explore the world of
animal and human communication, under such headings as
"When did a picture first tell a story," "Do languages change?" and
"How does a telephone work?"
1. Communication—Juvenile literature.
[1. Communication. 2. Questions and answers.]
I. Title. II. Series: I wonder why (New York, N.Y.)
P91.2.M39   1998   302.2—dc20   96-1371 CIP AC

ISBN 0-7534-5015-1
Printed in Italy

Series editor: Clare Oliver
Series designer: David West Children's Books
Author: Richard Mead
Consultant: Eryl Davies
Thanks to: Dr. Peter Narins, University of California
Cover illustration: Biz Hull (Artist Partners)
Cartoons: Tony Kenyon (BL Kearley)

CONTENTS

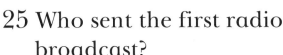

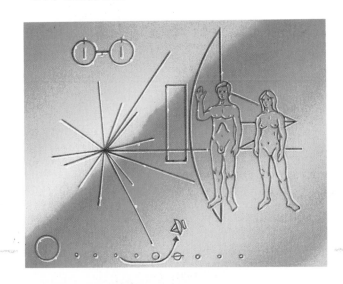

Why do we communicate?

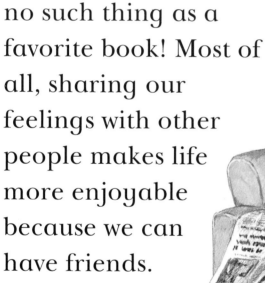

Communication is all about swapping information. If we didn't share our discoveries, we would have to learn everything from scratch. We'd have no way of knowing that fire burns, for example, until we'd been hurt. And there'd be no such thing as a favorite book! Most of all, sharing our feelings with other people makes life more enjoyable because we can have friends.

● Pictures are a good way of giving information. They can be understood by people who can't read, or who come from another country and don't know the language.

● Even before we learn how to speak, we can let others know when we want something!

4

How do we communicate?

When we're with someone, they use their voice and even their body language to communicate with us.

When someone is a long way away, they can get in touch on the telephone or send us a letter.

But people we have never even met communicate with us too—in the books they write, or the television programs and movies that they make.

● Burying a time capsule is a way to communicate across the centuries. Hopefully, it will help people in the future to piece together a picture of the past. What would you bury to show what your life is like?

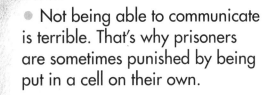

● Not being able to communicate is terrible. That's why prisoners are sometimes punished by being put in a cell on their own.

How do our senses help us to communicate?

We receive information about our world with our senses. Taste, touch, and smell tell us about things up close. And with our eyes and ears we can see and hear what is happening farther away.

● Sometimes you can't find out where things are by using your eyes. Then you have to use your other senses, such as touch or hearing.

● When you hurt yourself, messages are sent to your brain from tiny nerve endings in your skin. Feeling pain teaches us what will cause pain— so we don't do it again!

How do you talk with your fingers?

Sign language is a useful way to communicate if you are unable to hear or speak. Some signs stand for letters, but most words don't need spelling out—commonly-used ones have their own signs.

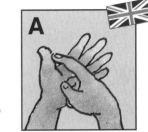

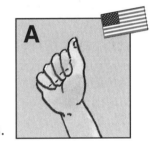

● Many blind people have someone else to be their eyes—a guide dog. It takes up to two years to train a guide dog, but it stays with its owner for the rest of its life.

● There are different sign languages, just as there are different spoken languages. American signs can usually be made with one hand but most British ones use two hands.

When does the nose know best?

Your nose can be very useful in dangerous situations. You might not be able to see or hear gas escaping, but you can certainly smell it. Your nose can stop you eating rotten food, too—try smelling a carton of milk that's past its sell-by date!

How does your body talk?

You don't need to talk to be understood—you can use your body. Just think how many different ways you can say hello to someone without speaking. Depending on where in the world you are, you might wave, shake hands, kiss cheeks, nod your head, give a big bear hug, slap palms in a high five, rub noses, or bow!

Why is a circle rude?

If you make a circle with your thumb and forefinger in France, it means "nothing"—or that something is worthless. But if you made the same gesture in the Middle East you'd be rudely telling someone to get lost! In Japan it stands for money. In the United States we'd use it to say "OK!"

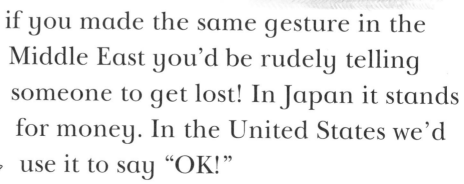

● If you tell a lie, you sometimes want to touch your face. It's as if you're trying to cover the lie coming from your mouth!

● If you're happy chatting to someone, you may find you copy their movements!

● If you feel nervous, you may fold your arms—making a barrier to protect yourself.

● You can greet people with your body. In Japan, it's polite to say hello by bowing from the waist, keeping your heels together.

9

Why don't animals talk like humans?

Nearly all animals have voices but none of them is as developed as the human voice. Your vocal cords, tongue, lips, teeth, and nose help you to make thousands of different sounds. Scientists have tried to teach apes to talk, but they can only copy a few simple words, as parrots do!

● Dolphins can make a wide range of noises, including squeaks, yelps, and clicks. If a dolphin is in distress, it makes a special two-note whistle. Dolphins nearby will recognize the sound and come to help.

Why do cats purr?

Cats can't talk, but they can still let us know how they feel. When cats purr, it usually means they're content. But sometimes they purr if they're hurt, to comfort themselves.

Who beats with their feet?

It can be very noisy in the rain forest, so Malaysian tree frogs don't croak to communicate. The females tap their toes on the leaves. A human wouldn't hear or feel this delicate vibration, but the male frogs can and come from all around to answer her call!

● Male antelopes rub their faces on plants and leave a smelly message for any other antelopes who come near. It says, "Stay away!"

● An adult firefly flashes its light on and off like a beacon to send messages to other fireflies. Some shine so brightly that you could read a book by them!

When did a picture first tell a story?

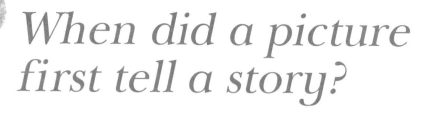

Over 20,000 years ago! Prehistoric people painted pictures on cave walls to tell stories— of a hunt, for example. These paintings tell us a story too. They tell us that prehistoric people could make paint from earth, charcoal, and plants.

What can a window teach you?

Stained-glass windows are used in churches to show scenes from the Bible. Long ago, very few people could read but they could look at the pictures and learn a story—such as the story of the Flood—in that way.

When artists paint portraits they often put in clues that tell us more about the person they are painting. Francisco Goya was a famous painter. He painted himself at work, and showed his favorite brushes and colors.

Why did knights have coats of arms?

When knights started to wear helmets, it was impossible to tell who was who, especially in battle! So every knight had a coat of arms—a design which decorated his shield, his lance and even his horse! This made sure no one on his own side would confuse him with the enemy.

Spray paint artists are sometimes hired to brighten up whole walls in run-down parts of a city. Not all graffiti is seen as art, though! Lots of money is spent every year cleaning up unwanted graffiti.

What is a dead language?

A dead language is one that no one speaks any more. Two thousand years ago, the Romans spoke Latin to one another. Although Latin is still taught in schools, it's no longer anyone's native language, so we call it dead.

Who started talking?

No one knows how or when people first spoke. They may have started by copying sounds around them, such as the whistling of the wind. One of the first words probably meant "attack." By communicating with words, humans could help each other more easily.

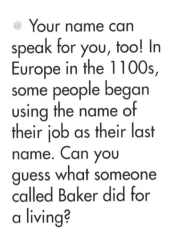

● Your name can speak for you, too! In Europe in the 1100s, some people began using the name of their job as their last name. Can you guess what someone called Baker did for a living?

● Life would be much simpler if we all spoke the same language. Hundreds of people have tried to invent one for everyone to use. Esperanto is the most popular—over 100,000 people use it!

Do languages change?

New words are being created all the time! Just think of all the new discoveries we've made during the last hundred years. Since we've been exploring space, the words spaceship, blast-off, and astronaut have all been invented.

● A speech synthesizer is a special machine for people who are unable to talk. You type the words you want to say on a keyboard, and the synthesizer says them out loud for you!

15

When did writing begin?

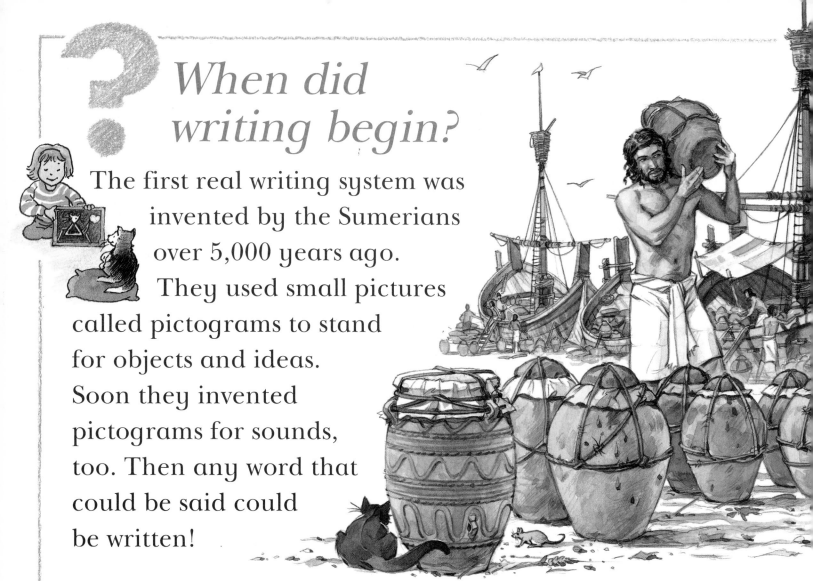

The first real writing system was invented by the Sumerians over 5,000 years ago. They used small pictures called pictograms to stand for objects and ideas. Soon they invented pictograms for sounds, too. Then any word that could be said could be written!

Who wrote on plants?

The ancient Egyptians did. They used the stalks of the papyrus plant, which was found by the Nile River. They cut the stalks into thin strips which they pressed together into sheets. Our word "paper" comes from "papyrus."

 Writing probably began so that people could keep a record of money and goods.

Who wrote in secret code?

Vikings wrote using runes, which were all drawn with straight lines. The word rune means "secret." Very few people could read a thousand years ago, and some of them believed that anyone who could understand the runes must have magical powers!

Why did typewriters drive you crazy?

People are often scared of new inventions. When the first typewriter went on sale in 1874, some doctors said that using one could make you go mad!

You can write on an electronic notepad as if it were an ordinary one, but with a special pen. Some of these notepads store information as you write it —others change your handwriting into neat type!

How does my letter reach my friend?

When you mail your letter, it gets taken from the mailbox to the nearest post office. There, it's sorted into a bag with other mail for the same area—so always write the address clearly! The bag with your letter in it is sent to the post office nearest your friend's house. From there, it gets delivered by hand!

● In remote places the mail is delivered by plane once a week.

● In 1860 the Pony Express began to carry mail between Saint Joseph, Missouri, and Sacramento, California, at top speed. It was a great success but lost its business a year later when people were able to send telegrams.

● Homing pigeons have been used to carry messages for thousands of years. Even the ancient Egyptians used them!

When was it bad to have friends?

Long ago, if you got mail you had to pay for the delivery—expensive if you were popular! In 1840 the British Post Office set up the system we know today, with stamps paid for by the sender. U.S. stamps first appeared in 1847.

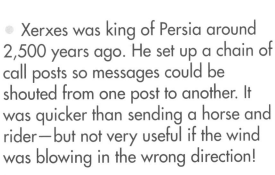

● Sending electronic mail by computer takes just seconds. No wonder traditional post is sometimes called "snail mail"!

● Xerxes was king of Persia around 2,500 years ago. He set up a chain of call posts so messages could be shouted from one post to another. It was quicker than sending a horse and rider—but not very useful if the wind was blowing in the wrong direction!

How are picture books printed?

Every picture in this book was printed using just four colors—black, yellow, magenta, and cyan. Magenta is a type of red and cyan is blue. As the paper runs through the printing press, each color is added separately to make different shades.

Cyan

Yellow

● In 1450, Johannes Gutenberg invented a new printing press with individual metal letters. The letters moved around and could be used repeatedly. Before that most books were copied by hand. The printing press was much faster!

● If you look at this page with a magnifying glass, you can see that all the colors are made from tiny black, yellow, magenta, and cyan dots. When they overlap, they mix together.

Magenta

Black

TONITE

WANTED
$1,000,000 Reward

LOST
FOUND

FOR SALE

Posters can be used to advertise, to warn people, or to ask for help.

How are newspapers made?

With the help of lots of people! Reporters write the stories, photographers take pictures of the story, and the editor decides which items should go in the paper. Designers put the words and pictures together on computer. Finally, a machine prints and folds the pages.

Photographer **Story** **Reporter** **Editor** **Designer** **Printer**

Why does the telephone ring?

The telephone rings to let you know that someone wants to speak to you! So if your friend dials your number, your phone rings. When you answer, an electric current carries your voice along the line and your friend hears you loud and clear.

● Today, most telephone exchanges connect calls automatically with computers.

● Telephone calls used to be connected by hand. An operator asked which telephone number you wanted and plugged in the correct wire.

How can glass link the world?

Optical fibers are hair-thin strands of glass, twisted into cable. They have been laid under all the oceans and act as highways for anything from phone calls to TV programs. Information travels along them at the speed of light.

● Telephones come in all shapes and sizes, from tiny mobiles to cartoon characters. But they all have two main parts—the transmitter you talk into and the receiver through which you hear.

Are phone lines just for voices?

Voices aren't the only things that travel along a phone line. With a videophone, you can see a picture of who's telephoning as well. With a fax, you can send letters, photos, and drawings. And computers use phone lines to communicate with one another, too!

● There are more than 100 million telephones in the United States. In Washington, D.C., there are more phones than people!

How does my stereo play a CD?

The bottom of a CD may look shiny, but it is covered with billions of tiny bumps. As the CD whizzes around inside your stereo, a laser beam shines on the bumps. The beam "reads" their pattern as a code, and then sends a message to the speakers to tell them exactly what sounds to make.

● The *Titanic* made its first and only voyage in 1912. As it sailed across the Atlantic, several other ships sent radio messages warning of icebergs ahead. The captain ignored them and the ship hit an iceberg and sank.

● Thomas Edison invented the first working record player. His first recording was "Mary had a little lamb."

Who sent the first radio broadcast?

The first true radio set that sent messages using radio waves was built by Guglielmo Marconi. But the person who proved the waves exist was the scientist Heinrich Hertz.

Marconi built a machine that could produce radio waves by making powerful electric sparks.

When a band plays in a studio, the engineer records the different instruments separately. The producer mixes them together to make the song.

When is communication out of this world?

Satellites are spacecraft that help us to communicate long distance. They send radio, TV, telephone, or computer signals from one country to another—in a quarter of a second! They pick up the signals from one of the great dishes on Earth called Earth Stations and beam them down to another station.

Solar panel
Communication satellites—called comsats for short—are powered by the Sun. Their solar panels change the Sun's energy into electricity.

Protective box
A box protects the delicate parts of the comsat from the Sun's heat.

● Calling all aliens! Space probes Pioneer I and II each carried a picture of a man and a woman and a map to show where Earth is in the solar system.

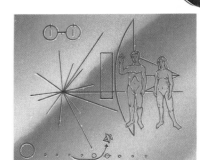

● The Hubble Space Telescope was taken into space by a shuttle. It sends pictures back to Earth and shows us stars whose light has taken ten billion years to reach us.

Are aliens trying to communicate with us?

There's no proof that extraterrestrials exist at all. But just in case there are any trying to get in touch with us, monster-sized radio telescopes are picking up radio waves from space. There have been no alien broadcasts yet though!

Dishes
Comsats have several dishes, each one pointing at an Earth Station or another comsat's dish. This is so they can send and receive many different types of signal.

How does the news appear on TV?

Journalists can send words and pictures back to the newsroom, even from remote areas. They use a portable satellite transmitter to beam their report up to a comsat in space, and the comsat bounces it down to the TV station. So we see what is going on—within a second of it happening!

News stations have journalists on hand in every corner of the globe. That way, they're ready to report the news as it happens.

Who put the noise into silent movies?

The first movies didn't have any sound. Pianists played along with them to set the mood. The first long film with sound was *The Jazz Singer*, in 1927. It was a huge hit, and silent movies soon disappeared.

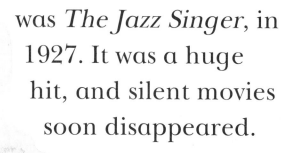

In the future, TV sets will have LCDs—Liquid Crystal Displays—like the screens of a hand-held computer game. Your TV could be as thin as a framed picture !

With a camcorder, you can make your own movie. You can also use one to send video messages to friends and relations who live far away.

You might have seen security cameras in stores or outside buildings. If a crime takes place, the police can play back the film to see what happened.

Is virtual reality just for fun?

● Architects can use virtual reality to walk around a building they have designed —before it's been built!

When you put on a virtual reality (VR) helmet, you could be exploring a spooky castle or zooming into space. A computer makes it seem as if you've traveled to a different place. But virtual reality can also be used to teach people how to drive, or to help student doctors practice operations —without harming anyone!

● VR helmets are being used to make new medicines. They make tiny atoms appear as colored balls. Scientists can string together different combinations of balls until they find a set of ingredients that works.

● You can even shop on your computer! You choose from pictures on your screen, money is taken from your bank account, and the items are delivered to your door.

Why do we use computers?

Computers can store millions of times more information than we can. They let us swap information with each other, too. Using a machine called a modem, one computer can be connected to another along a phone line. The network of linked computers is called the Internet, and users say they are surfing the Net!

● The Internet was started by the U.S. government for communicating in wartime. Even if one computer on the Net is destroyed, the rest can still communicate.

Index

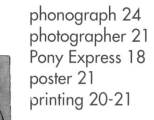